# Introduction

Welcome to the world of crochet! This guide is designed to introduce you to the basics of crocheting and provide you with the knowledge and skills to embark on your crochet journey. Whether you're a complete beginner or have some experience, this guide will help you understand the fundamentals, learn essential techniques, and explore various crochet patterns.

Begin by understanding the basics of crocheting, including its history and why it's a popular hobby. Discover the benefits of crocheting as a creative outlet, stress reliever, and a way to make beautiful and functional items. Learn about the differences between crocheting and knitting and why you might choose one over the other.

Explore the essential tools needed for crocheting, including crochet hooks, yarn, stitch markers, and other accessories. Understand how to choose the right hook and yarn for your projects, and learn about different types of yarn fibers and weights.

Master the proper techniques for holding your yarn and hook while crocheting. Follow step-by-step instructions to learn the basic crochet stitches, such as slip knot, chain stitch, single crochet, half double crochet, and treble crochet. Practice these stitches until you feel comfortable with them, as they form the foundation for more complex patterns.

Discover how to join yarn and fasten off your work, allowing you to change colors or finish your projects neatly. Learn how to read crochet patterns, including understanding crochet terms and abbreviations. Familiarize yourself with common crochet measurements and terms used in patterns.

Explore a collection of 25 crochet patterns that are essential for beginners. From lacy stitches to textured designs, these patterns will help you expand your skills and create a variety of beautiful projects. Learn how to make items like pineapple lace, beanies, scarves, blankets, and more.

Understand the importance of caring for your crochet products. Learn how to properly wash and store your crocheted items to ensure their longevity and maintain their quality. Discover tips for selecting the right cleaning methods and storing techniques based on the type of yarn used.

With this guide, you'll gain the confidence to start crocheting and create wonderful projects of your own. Remember, practice is key, and with each stitch, you'll improve your skills and develop your unique crocheting style. Enjoy the process, embrace your creativity, and have fun as you delve into the world of crochet!

Get your hooks and yarn ready, and let's begin your crochet journey with this book. Happy crocheting!

# Contents

# Chapter 1: Understanding the Basics of Crocheting

The word 'crochet' has been derived from another word that is originally of French-origin, 'crochet,' which is a diminutive of 'croche,' which, in turn, comes from another word of Germanic origin 'croc,' both meaning' hook.' Most of us have come across crochet in the form of either accessories or apparel, but crochet isn't the name of the fabric itself; but it is basically the process of creating that very fabric by a certain method. Crochets can be a very interesting break from the monotony of items that we use every day. Crochets are created by taking different loops of yarns or threads or strands of other materials and interlocking them with the help of a hook. Crochet threads are usually made from cotton, having a smaller diameter and denser pile than the regular yarn.

## History of Crocheting

It was in 19th century Ireland that crocheting was introduced as a form of relief method for famine during the great Irish famine (1845-1849). It was a method for the poor to earn some money. This craft of crocheting reached America with the migration of the people of Ireland. Crocheting then saw a surge in its craft during the 1960s, when an interest in the home crafts rose in people, and particularly in the United States. The new generation of America saw a rise in people's interest in crocheting with bright and beautiful flowers during the 1960s and 1970s. Then there was a brief period of decline of the popularity of crochets, but again during the 21st century, a change in people's choices led to them wanting materials of bright colors. The best part is, nowadays, the materials for crocheting are very easily available online, and the art of crocheting can actually be self-taught through books and other sources at our disposal.

The fashion world has had a revival of this art of crocheting since 2011, and many designers and international brands have made intensive use of crochet techniques to enhance their designs and sales.

An interesting fact about crocheting is that in Denmark, it is known as *haekling*; in Sweden, it is known as *virkning*; in Holland, they call crocheting as *haken,* and in Norway, it is known as *hekling.* A researcher named Lis Paludan, who is from Denmark, during the search for the origin of crocheting, gave us three very interesting theories. Firstly, Paludan says that there is a possibility that crocheting originated in Arabia, and then it spread eastward to Tibet and westward to Spain and finally to Mediterranean countries. According to another theory, the earliest pieces of evidence of crocheting can be found in South America. It is said that some primitive tribe has been found to use crochet methods to adorn their puberty rites. And lastly, early examples have been found in China, where three- dimensional dolls were made by using crochet methods.

## Why Should We Use Crocheting As a Hobby?

It is now a well-known fact that arts and crafts, when used as a hobby, not only helps us grow a positive outlook it also helps in a healing process. Along with being a fun pastime, such hobbies are hugely beneficial as they often have a therapeutic effect on us. Similarly, there are numerous positive and useful benefits of crocheting that we should be aware of.

It is really surprising to know that learning a new craft like crocheting can very extremely helpful for strengthening one's concentration abilities as well as help sharpening eye power. Along with these, a helpful habit such as crocheting will also help in relieving problems of stress as our mind gets preoccupied in doing something fruitful that takes all our concentration, so quite naturally, one will find it to be a way to lessen the stress that is otherwise causing a problem. It has also been reported that other serious mental health issues like depression, which otherwise might need medicinal aid to be kept under control, can also be benefitted by cultivating a habit like crocheting. Crocheting also is hugely beneficial for reducing the risk of Alzheimer's disease. The best thing about a hobby like crocheting is that not only does it have a positive impact on the concerned person who is inculcating the hobby, it also helps the other people surrounding that person. For people who visit group therapy sessions, crocheting can be a really good option to take up as a hobby when the focus is not completely on you.

**Crocheting Reduces Insomnia**

It might be unknown to many, but keeping one's mind and body in a calm situation can be helpful for a problem like insomnia. Crocheting helps one to achieve that calm state of mind easily. It helps to concentrate on one thing completely, which will help the concerned person to have a better sleep.

## Helps in Bringing Down Anxiety

Crocheting helps a person to bring down his anxiety and stress level to a great extent. Taking your mind off all the negativities that are pressurizing you at the moment and investing that energy into something completely productive is actually a great way to bring down one's stress levels.

## Reduces the Risk of Alzheimer's

Crocheting can effectively reduce the risk of Alzheimer's by almost thirty to fifty percent. A problem like Alzheimer's can be kept under control if the patient engages in cognitive exercises that help stimulate one's mind. That is exactly what crocheting helps one with. The concerned person will be greatly helping boost up his memory by either challenging oneself to learn a new stitching method or by simply trying to remember the basics of a pattern.

## Pumps Up One's Self-Esteem

By working on a project, be it something you are making for yourself, or making it as a gift to give to someone, just the act of creating something beautiful by one's own potential, is a great way to give oneself a positive push in the right direction. At the same time, everyone appreciates a beautiful gift and more so if it's a hand-made one. The genuine appreciation that one usually receives after getting a gift like that is further a great medium to feel happy with oneself and thereby increasing one's self-esteem.

## Helps One to Regain Control

Cultivating a hobby like crocheting actually helps you become more organized about your work and day-to-day life on the whole. It gives you an overall feeling and satisfaction of being in control of things around you. So, whether you feel that things are too difficult to control otherwise, the sense of productive security that something like crocheting provided you with will definitely help you gain the confidence to put back things in order. During that creative process, whatever you decide, will be the thing that happens. And it is your decisions that will, in turn, create something beautiful. This helps in restoring One's sense of low self-esteem.

## Helpful in Postponing Dementia

It has been proved in several studies that practicing a craft that is as productive as crocheting can also prove immensely helpful in postponing dementia that occurs with age in people. For those people, who have already started facing the pangs of dementia, crocheting can actually help reduce further damage and soothe the mind. Practices like knitting and crocheting are neuroprotective, which helps lessen the effects of dementia.

## Promotes Relaxation

Many people find the act of praying to be healing and to have many health benefits. A very effective way to put this into practice is to pray while doing one's prayers. This enhances the power of the body to relax and reduce problems of getting irritated easily. If someone has the habit of getting restless often, crocheting can be a very helpful hobby because the practice of sitting stable in a place while concentrating on one particular job will teach the concerned person exactly what he lacks.

### Helps Deal With Grief

Crocheting can become very helpful in reducing your pain and process grief. It takes our mind off those things which are causing us pain, be it even for a short time. So, while we are engaged in doing something beautiful and productive, we get clarity, and with that, we can effectively process our grief. This will help us make rational decisions further.

### Effective Way of Group Therapy

*Lastly*, crocheting also acts as a form of group therapy. While working in a group, a craft like this will most definitely act as a kind of ice-breaker, and it establishes a sense of community among the members that benefit the group hugely. The feeling of belonging to a community is something that many of us lacks and need as well. Something as simple as being a part of the local knit-ins or crochet-in-public groups can be of more help than we can imagine. Participating in fiber fairs or such related events can be a great opportunity for meeting new people, exchanging ideas, encouraging one another, and also showcasing one's talents. Such meetings could also be an opportunity to get ideas of start-ups with an inclination of one's work, reaching a wider audience. This is one such hobby that is easily welcomed and appreciated by people of all generations. So crocheting might also be helpful as a tool to bond with people of other generations.

## Crocheting vs. Knitting

Knitting and crocheting are both very exciting when someone pursues it as a hobby. These constantly inspire a person to create new projects by employing new techniques. It can very well be that a person prefers one over the other or equally enjoys both. Both the crafts need a hook or what we know as a needle that is used to manipulate the threads or yarns to make toys, blankets, sweaters, or hats. Though these two yarn crafts share many similarities, yet on various levels, they are very different from each other as well. Crocheting and knitting use different hooks or needles, and the techniques involved are also very different, thereby producing different results. That being said, knitting and crocheting both require a person to have a keen sense of color so as to create something beautiful while at the same time maintaining a balance of colors for the product to actually look nice. Both these crafts need a certain level of hand-eye coordination, without which the desired design might be a lot difficult to achieve. The person has to have a basic knowledge and affinity for fiber, otherwise taking up a project and completing it might be very strenuous work. Not all fibers are fit for all designs. And finally, the thing that goes without saying is that be it for knitting or for crocheting; it is of utmost importance for the person to have the patience and zeal to actually complete a project once it has been taken up. Both these crafts require a steady amount of patience and cannot be done if one has an attitude of getting irritated fast.

In crochet, the stitches usually take the shape of knots, while in knitting, the yarns, after being stitched, take up a 'v' shape. If we look into the process of knitting, a pair of long needles are used to form the loops, and then these long needles are used to move a set of loops from one needle to the other. It is on the needle that the stitches are held. In the case of crocheting, however, a single hook is used in order to hook one loop with another directly on the piece. Some might be of the opinion that it is for this very reason; doing crochet work is easier than knitting. That is the reason, for those who are still at a beginner level, they can very easily take up crocheting if they are looking for versatility and convenience in the next project that they take up.

Knitting needles are often four dual-pointed needles used to work in circles, or they might also be circular needles, that is, two knitting needles that are joined by a kind of flexible pipe. These are completely different from the hooks that are used in crocheting. For those who have a time factor to consider, crocheting might be a more welcome option because knitting definitely takes more time. While choosing your fabric, something that needs to be kept in mind is that the threads or yarns used in crochet are thicker than the threads used in knitting. Crocheting in circles and crocheting straight both requires very less effort, which is why many people choose it over knitting because while knitting straight is a fairly easy job, but knitting in circles is an extremely cumbersome thing. The same goes for using color threads. Changing colors in knitting horizontal is an easy thing to do while in crocheting, be it vertically or horizontally, changing colors while creating a pattern is actually very easy.

What many people don't know is that crocheting, as compared to knitting, is much more beneficial for our physical health. The craft of knitting and the hand movements required can actually put a lot of effort on our shoulders. As a result, a prolonged session of knitting is not good for our shoulders. Crocheting, on the other hand, has no such negative impacts on the body. It's much more sympathetic towards our health. The two main kinds of stitches that are used in knitting are known as *knit* and *purl*. But when we consider the craft of crocheting, there are four kinds of stitches that are generally employed. These four kinds of stitches are known as *single Crochet, half-double Crochet, double crochet,* and *triple crochet.* For those who have a fair idea about knitting and crocheting, it is natural to feel that the texture of a knitted fabric is very smooth, especially when it has been knitted without any pattern. A crocheted item will generally be way less stretchable when we compare it with a portion of a knitted item.

# Tools That Are Essential For Crocheting

Down below are listed a few basic but absolutely necessary tools that are required for anyone who decides to begin with crocheting.

## Yarn

The first job is to buy proper yarn. Buying yarn is an extremely enjoyable work that will invariably help you to lift up your mood. Those beautiful colors are sure to take your stress away. However, yarns are usually made up of various different products. They can be made from both natural fibers and synthetic fibers. They can be either in filament or staple form. The filament is the fiber of great length that includes natural fiber silk as well as synthetic fibers. So quite naturally, different crocheting projects will require different kinds of yarns. Hence, it's important to do a bit of research regarding the kind of yarn one needs for that particular work before actually going to buy the yarn.

## Crochet Hooks

The second thing that one needs to buy is the crochet hook. As for these crochet hooks, they, too, are made up of different materials. Each type of hooks has its specific benefits and problems, be it in their use or price, or comfort. Average basic crochet hooks are available for beginners who are usually of size G or of size H. these are usually made up of bamboo and are the most common choices. The next thing to be kept in mind is the hook throat. They usually have a tapered or inline throat that is based on the flatness of the head of the hook. Your choice of buying the hook thus depends on the design and material being used as the flatness of the head will then differ. Another thing that needs to be kept in mind is that the hook will be different when the crocheting is being done with threads rather than wool. Crocheting with thread will require a much smaller hook. There are many people who suffer from arthritis or might find it uncomfortable to work with regular hooks for a long time. Hence, there are *ergonomic crochet hooks* available with larger handles that are specially shaped to facilitate the crafting process.

## Scissors

The next important tool essential for crocheting is scissors. You just cannot go without it. Sewing scissors usually have different types because they have different functions to fulfill. Scissors are of many types. Be it for embroidery or rotary, or pinking, each one has different features of its own. Hence it becomes essential to choose the correct one.

Along with hooks, a darning needle is something else that is very important for crocheting. The regular needle generally has a very small eye for thread insertion. But when it comes to darning needles, they have big eyes as, during crocheting, it is yarn or thick threads that are being used. It helps to crochet the ends of one's work together.

## Measuring Tapes

Be it any craft; it is always more desirable and more soothing to the eyes if that work has been done with precision. The same goes for a handcraft like crocheting. As it usually has intricate designs made by knots of various colors, a person needs to be precise and neat for sure so as to help project the designs clearly. It is for this very reason that taking measurements becomes a clever thing to do. So, measuring tape is very useful. If, while keeping the design in mind, the person also measures the area available and design pattern, then it becomes easier to bring forth the intended design as well, along with the work consuming less time due to prior planning. The end result also is neat and beautiful.

## Crochet Organizer

Something that can cause a real problem is when you lose your crocheting tools, as needles and hooks are prone to get lost often. So, instead of hunting down the hooks every time you decide to sit with a crocheting project, it is better to make yourself a crochet organizer where you can easily store all your threads and hooks and needles. This will help you remain organized, saving you the trouble of losing time in hunting your hooks down.

## Stitch Markers

A very useful tool for beginners and veterans alike is stitch markers. They are very cute clips, easily available in the market, used to keep a mark on the starting and ending point of One's design or pattern. This makes the work further easier, especially if one is crocheting something in a circular pattern. The circular pattern is a bit complex and might be a bit difficult for people to do. Hence, something like a stitch marker helps in pointing out from the area where we need to start without getting angry.

## Row Counters

Digital row counter devices are easily available nowadays, which helps in keeping a count of the number of rows you have already created. It basically saves a lot of time. So, if you are a beginner at crocheting, do give some thought to whether you want to buy it or not, as the initial days of grasping the art might be a bit confusing. You could opt for a digital row counter, which you can easily wear on your wrist like a normal watch. These also come with an LED display in place of sliding numbers manually. Buying a manual row counter is also an option as the cost is not much different. That being said, it is not absolutely necessary to buy a row counter if you are capable of keeping track in your head. However, it's not a bad investment as well if you decide to have one.

## Yarn Organizer

An unavoidable hazard that comes with crocheting is keeping all your yarns in place. No matter how much you try, they are bound to slip here and there, creating a tangled mess. So, if you are thinking of taking up crocheting as a hobby and yarns are going to become a part of your life, then it is advisable to get for yourself a yarn organizer. It will have different shelves where you can neatly store not only all your yarns but also your books and hooks of crocheting. Portable yarn organizers are also available for those who wish to carry their crocheting while traveling.

## Crochet Design Books

Stitch patterns can be very helpful for beginners to follow. There is no shame in taking up a design or getting inspired by one that you have seen on some online platform, as long as your work has been honest. Thus, anyone can easily search the internet to get new ideas for stitch patterns. Crochet books are also easily available for anyone interested in doing this as a hobby, where extensive information regarding crocheting is available. I sincerely thank you for choosing this one as your guide.

Crocheting is a lot of fun. It is such a hobby that gives you pleasure, inspires your creativity, and soothes your soul. For everyone thinking of taking it up seriously, hopefully, enough information has been provided here for you all to give it a go.

# Chapter 2: Tips on Holding Your Yarn and Hook While Crocheting

If you are a newbie in the field of crocheting, then it is very important for you to consider if you are holding your hook and yarn in an effective manner while you crochet. It is really easy to make a mistake when it comes to how you deal with the yarn and hook, and an ineffective method could prove really poor for your crocheting. Here are some easy to follow tips and tricks on holding your yarn and hook while crocheting, which are bound to help you out and make things a lot more convenient for you:

- Make sure to place the yarn in your hand, which is less dominant. Make sure you find a holding style that is comfortable for you because you would not be able to do it for very long otherwise. The posture will depend on which hand is your dominant hand, but make sure it gives you enough room for both movement and rest.

- The yarn hand will be controlling your grip and the tension in which the yarn is being fed into the hook (which will be controlled by your dominant hand). The yarn tension is what will be determining how tight or how loose the end result of your crocheting is going to be.

- The *Traditional Method* of holding your hook and yarn is where you hold both your yarn and crochet in your non-dominant hand while you hold the hook in the dominant hand. The hook is held in a posture which makes it angle like a pencil. Then, you must hold the yarn in between your thumb and forefinger while you work on the ball of yarn using the other three fingers. Next, you need to bend the fourth finger around the yarn to secure it in its position. The grip needs to be firm, but not too firm, as then the yarn would not be able to move freely. If you feel like the yarn is moving too fast and you cannot control it, then you can try using the little finger of your non-dominant hand by wrapping it around the yarn twice in order to slow down the flow and gain extra control over the yarn.

- There is an *Alternative Method*, where you can use only your non-dominant hand for most of the movement required while your dominant hand stays completely still. It is only advisable for you if you have some difficulties in free and continuous movement in the stance of your dominant hand.

- Another useful method, known as the *One-Handed Method*, can also be very helpful. In this method, you have to hold both your hook and your yarn in your dominant hand (in the same way in which you might be holding the needle and yarn while you are knitting). Next, you must hold the crochet between the thumb and the first finger of your non-dominant hand and bring the hook around the yarn in the direction opposite to the one you would normally knit in, which means, if you are crocheting, you will need to move the hook from back to front.

- There is another method, called the *Left-Handed Method*, where you just swap the hand in which you are holding the yarn to the opposite side. This way, all the other techniques will be just used in reverse, based on which is your dominant hand.

- If you are using the *Over and Under Hold* to hold your yarn, you will need to position the yarn under your dominant little finger and over your ring finger. Next, put the yarn under your middle finger, and move it along your index finger, after which you will have to pull the yarn down along the insides of your palm. Next, grip the yarn using your ring and little finger to hold it in a firm position.

- You can also try out the *Pointer Hold* or the *Pinky Hold,* as both of these are really convenient grips if you are having any problems with easily working out any of the other techniques that have already been mentioned here. For these techniques, place the yarn under your palm, positioning the tail end of the yarn between either your pinky finger or your pointer finger (depending on which hold you are using) and your ringer finger. Loop the yarn around your pinky/pointer finger and make a loop, and carry on with the process by working the yarn around the loop.

- Another holding technique that is really easy to practice and get used to is known as the *Single Loop Hold*. If you are using this, then you need to put your palm face down, putting the tail end of the yarn over the ring finger. Next, pull the yarn down slowly along the inner edge of the palm and grip the yarn with your little and ring fingers. In the same manner, carry on with the process, but try alternating the tension to find out which works the best for you- depending on how tight or loose you want your finished product to be.

- Some of the other most widely used techniques used for your yarn are (a) *The Crochet Slip Knot*, (b) *The Loose Yarn Technique*, and (c) *The Forefinger Hold Technique*.

It can be really tough to initially figure out how to hold your yarn and hook if you are a beginner, and that is completely alright, and there is no need to lose heart over it! Everyone needs some time to ease into the process and find a grip and a technique that works for them. But constant practice and a lot of patience are what will actually help you ace it and get comfortable with your crocheting. Not just efficiency but comfort is also very important, so while picking your preferred technique, you also need to factor in which stance makes you feel the most comfortable, and that will help you get the best results!

# Chapter 3: Learning the Basic Crocheting Steps

This chapter will help you to learn the basic steps that you need to learn if you are a beginner in crocheting. These steps are necessary for you to learn if you want to learn harder and complicated patterns later. Let us see some of the basic crocheting steps.

## Slip Knot

In almost every crochet pattern, the first thing you need to do is to make a slip knot. In case you are working from a crochet pattern, you can use the crochet hook and yarn outlined by the pattern instructions. In case you are just learning crochet, it is better if you start with a mid-size yarn (wool, cotton, or acrylic yarn) and hook (H/8 or G/6). Make sure to choose a yarn that is not too fuzzy and is of bright or light color. It is wiser to go for basic yarns while starting off because, in the initial days, you will need to see the stitches. There are various ways of making a slip knot, and some are quite confusing as well. Let me focus on only one simple method which is easy to understand for beginners.

*Hold the Hook and Yarn*

Take out a four-inch tail of the yarn in the front side, keeping the yarn ball (working strand) backward. Hold your yarn in between your index finger and thumb. Make sure that your yarn is able to flow over your index finger freely. Use your ring and middle fingers to support the strands of yarn. In your right hand, grasp the hook using either a knife grip or a pencil grip. Keep your fingers relaxed so that they can move freely. Also, make sure that your grip is tight enough for maintaining precise control over your hook. The crochet hook should face upwards, and then slip it between your index finger and the yarn for the beginning.

### Create A Loop on the Hook

Make sure to not let go of the yarn strands in your left hand. Then lift the hook above your left hand. Then with the help of your right index finger, try holding the top of the draped yarn on your crochet hook. The head of the crochet hook needs to be rotated clockwise under the right hand and then again back to the starting position. You are basically turning the hook in a circle. This is going to twist the yarn strands, and a loose loop will be formed on the hook. Note that it is not yet secured.

### Yarn Over Hook

Prepare your left-hand fingers, to begin with, crocheting. Start with pinching the yarn tail between your thumb and middle finger. Insert your index finger between the yarn strands and then up to the back. This is to make sure that the working yarn can be easily manipulated as it unwinds from the yarn ball. For creating proper tension, the yarn strand should form a loop over your index finger and pass between the other fingers. You can use your left hand to wrap the yarn over the hook, starting from behind to the top. You can also use your right hand to manipulate the hook for doing the same thing. This is called 'yarn over' or 'yarn round hook.' It will feel a little awkward and complicated at first, but with more and more practice, it will feel natural.

### Draw the Yarn through a Loop

Try drawing the yarn through the twisted loop present on the crochet hook, using the head of the hook. The yarn will pass through the loop, and then a loose slip knot will be formed on the hook. It should not be excessively tight but snug. So, finally, you are done with making a slip knot. You are now ready to start making chain stitches.

*Tips*

The beginning slip knot, in crochet, doesn't count as a stitch. In knitting, the first slip knot creates a stitch. It is different in the case of crochet. When you follow the instructions of the crochet pattern and count the stitches of the foundation chain, make sure not to count the first slip knot.

## Chain Stitch

The next thing that you need to do after making a slip knot is to make a series of chain stitches. They are responsible for building the foundation on which you will be building the rest of your crocheting project. This is one of the various essential stitches that a beginner should know.

*Hold the Hook and Yarn*

After making a slip knot, grasp it using the middle finger and thumb of your left hand. Make sure that the slip knot faces you. The working yarn should flow between your middle finger and index finger, across your palm, and then again back in between your little finger and ring finger. It may feel a little awkward in the beginning, but it will help you to build the required tension in the yarn as you progress with making stitches and needing more yarn. Grasp the crochet hook using a knife grip or a pencil grip in your right hand. The hook should face upwards. Make sure to grip the hook tight enough for maintaining the control and also loose enough for moving it easily.

*Yarn Over Hook*

Make a loop over the hook with the working yarn from back to front. Use your left hand to wrap the yarn over the hook from behind to the top. You may also use your right hand to manipulate the hook for doing the same.

*Draw Through Loop*

Rotate the crochet hook counterclockwise by one-quarter turn while looping the yarn for preparing it for hooking. If required, you can turn it more. Your end goal is to make every move fluid and precise. Pull down the hook and then pull it through the loop currently present on the hook. After this, you can easily complete the step by returning it back to its original position.

*Make a Chain*

You have just made one chain stitch. For making another chain stitch, you have to yarn over the hook at first and then draw up a loop. Do this process and repeat as many times as required. As you progress with the crocheting, move your index finger and thumb up the newly made chain stitches. Make sure to stay one or two stitches away from the loop present on the hook. It will allow you to have more control and also help you to maintain a better tension while making the stitches, i.e., not too loose, not too tight. As your work progresses, you will find a rhythm in rotating the hook. You will continue to yarn over and then rotate it back while drawing through the loop. When you find your rhythm, the process will become faster and easier.

*Tips*

Start counting with the first chain stitch and end counting with the one before the hook. Practice more and more so that your chain stitches become even, smooth, and moderately tight. Everyone's crocheting technique is different. There are various ways in which you can position the hook and hold the yarn. I only explained one way of doing it. If you are not comfortable with it, don't hesitate to modify your working way to the one that suits you the best. If you are using a non-stretchy yarn or a cotton yarn, you will need to use a hook that is one size larger than the hook you use for the rest of your crocheting project. If you see that your foundation chain is way too tight, then don't hesitate to use a larger hook.

## Single Crochet

One of the most important stitches that you need to know is single crochet. A lot of crochet projects and patterns involve single crochet stitches. Single crochet is very easy to learn, and once you learn it, there are infinite ways in which you can use it. You can work it in spirals or rounds, in rows, in combination with other stitches in different variations, in various parts of the stitch for various effects, as edging, etc.

*Insert the Crochet Hook*

After forming the foundation chain stitches, you need to insert the hook through the first chain. Then directly insert the hook into the single crochet stitch below it in the row for making the second row and so on. Then you have to slide the crochet hook under both the loops present on the top of the chain. Some patterns demand you to only work through one loop and some both loops. But if you are in a state of confusion, go for two loops straight away.

*Yarn over and Grab It*

When the crochet hook is at a place, start to prepare for drawing up a loop. Then wrap the yarn over the hook and grab it. After practicing these steps, you will reach a point when you are able to do it automatically, even without a gap between the two steps. When you insert the hook into the yarn, it will grab the yarn instantly.

*Draw Up the Loop*

Pull the working yarn and hook through the loops. Then you will have two loops on your hook.

*Again Yarn Over*

Again wrap the yarn around the hook and then hook the yarn.

*Draw Your Yarn through Both the Loops*

Draw the yarn and hook through both the loops on your hook. With this, the single crochet stitch is completed. Then one loop remains on the hook. This is the starting point of your next stitch. Repeat these steps as many times as required for creating the additional single crochet stitches across the row.

*Tips*

If you are a beginner and are working your crochet in rows, then the first row can be quite challenging. If you are facing trouble to work on the first row of the single crochet, seek help from an experienced crocheter. Ask him to make the first several rows for you. After that, you may continue crocheting. When you see that the first few rows are complete, you will find it way easier to work.

## Half Double Crochet

Half double crochet is simple, beautiful, and versatile. It is a basic stitch that a beginner should master. When compared with the double crochet, this one is shorter, but if you compare it with the single crochet stitch, then the half double crochet is taller. There is another thing that you should know about the half double crochet – it also acts as a foundation stitch in many projects. A smaller height and a third loop are created by a unique difference.

*Choose a Crochet Hook and Yarn*

There are so many stitching patterns where half double crochet is required. As far as the yarn and hook are concerned, you can choose any type to work on a half double crochet. But in any case, before you start any stitching pattern, always look for the requirements because sometimes, in order to get the exact, finished look, you need certain types of yarns and hooks to work with. But if you are not following any particular pattern, then your first step is to choose your yarn. Once you do that, you can read the instructions on the packet of the yarn and then choose your hook accordingly. If you are a beginner, then use an H size crochet hook and worsted weight yarn.

*Make a Foundation Chain*

All of the crochet patterns begin with a slip knot. Now, you simply have to make a foundation chain by following the instructions given to you. The foundation chain is also popularly referred to as the starting chain. The length of the foundation chain can be anything you want. The chain length usually depends on the particular project you are working on, so make sure you check that.

*Start in the Correct Chain*

Choose a chain that is after three chains from the hook and then make the first double crochet into the foundation chain. You will need to start with a turning chain if you are crocheting in rows. The height of your crochet stitch will determine the height of the turning chain.

*Insert the Crochet Hook after Yarning Over*

You have to make the first half double crochet. Before you insert the hook into the stitch, you have to yarn over. This step is mandatory if you want to do the double crochet stitch. But if you want the single crochet, then before inserting the hook, you can skip the yarning over step. Any stitch increases in height whenever you decide to yarn over, and thus, a half double crochet is taller in size when compared to the single crochet.

*Yarn Over and Pull through the Stitch*

Pull the yarn through the stitch after yarning over again. You will have three loops then.

*Yarn Over and Pull through the Loops*

Yarn over once again and then pull the yarn through all three loops. Then you will have the first half double crochet stitch.

*Complete the row*

For each half double crochet, repeat these steps. Work across the foundation chain's rows and also across every stitch of all subsequent rows.

*Decreasing and Increasing in Half Double Crochet*

Whenever the pattern asks you to perform consistent rows, using the basic half double crochet in such cases is very easy. But in the case of patterns where you have to shape the project in a particular way, you have to be aware of how you can increase or decrease the half double crochet. For increasing, you need to make an extra Half Double Crochet stitch after already making one. Where or how to do this is dependent on the crochet pattern. If you want to increase at the row's end, then you will have to crochet two Half Double Crochet stitches in your final stitch, rather than to work on the one you usually do.

For decreasing, you have to insert the hook into the stitch after yarning over. Again yarn over and then pull through. After this, yarn over again and insert the crochet hook into the next stitch. Finally, yarn over, and then you have to pull through all the five loops.

*Tips*

The double crochet stitch can be replaced by the half double crochet stitch in many patterns for a shorter design. Half double stitches are preferred for edging the blankets beautifully. You can change the appearance of the simple half double crochet stitch by working only into one of the loops and not into both the loops.

# Treble Crochet

Various crochet designs involve long stitches. These designs involve treble crochet. This is not at all tough. It is one of the basic stitches that a beginner needs to learn while starting off with crocheting. It takes just 5 minutes to make it. This is the next basic stitch after the double crochet. It is used in crochet patterns frequently. If you know how to do a double crochet, then treble crochet will not be that hard for you to learn. It is used when a long stitch is required in a crochet design. It is taller than the double crochet but is based on the same design.

*Crocheting the Treble Crochet Stitches*

First, yarn over the hook twice, and then take the hook and put it inside the next stitch. Before drawing the yarn through the stitch again, yarn over. You will see two loops on your yarn. Loop the yarn over the hook and then draw it through all the loops. This will give you a total of 3 loops on the hook. Here, you have to first draw the yarn through the first two loops, but before that, don't forget to yarn over. Yarn over again. You still have two more loops on the hook, and in order to finish this, draw the yarn through those remaining two loops. This completes your one treble crochet.

*Double Treble Crochet*

Yarn over the hook three times and then insert the hook into the next stitch. Yarn over the hook and then draw the yarn through the stitch, i.e., the five loops on the hook. Loop yarn over hook and then draw it through two loops. Now, four loops are remaining on the hook. Yarn over the hook and then draw it through the two loops. Repeat this process two more times. Double treble crochet is completed.

*Triple Treble Crochet*

Yarn over the hook four times. Insert the hook into the next stitch and then draw through the loops, i.e., the six loops present on the hook. Yarn over and then draw through the two loops. Repeat this process four more times. Triple treble crochet is completed.

*Tips*

When the treble crochet row ends, in order to turn, you have to chain four. Measure the height of the remaining stitches in the row because your turning chain's height will depend on it. Often, when you are making a front post stitch o a back post, the treble crochet stitch is used—some other designs where this sticth is used are crochet cables and the basketweave stitch. In advanced crochet, it is often used to crochet in the remaining loop (a loop which is made when a stitch is done in the back loop only) of one stitch that is situated several rows below.

## Joining the Yarn

If you are working on a big project, for example, a big scarf, a clothing item, or a blanket, you won't be able to finish the entire project with just one ball of yarn. This is where joining the yarn comes in. There are various indispensable ways for joining the yarn in crochet. In this guide, I will be talking about four such ways. If you are not comfortable with these methods, go ahead and search for other ways and choose the one that suits you the best.

*Join a New Yarn with the Last Yarn over of One Stitch*

It is the quickest and easiest way to join yarn in crochet. In this process, you just have to grab your new yarn and continue crocheting seamlessly. This process is very effective in case you are planning to change yarn color, like in some methods of the fair isle crochet and in the tapestry crochet. It also has some adverse effects.

It is not as secure as the rest of the joining methods, i.e., the yarns can come apart easily. You also need to weave in ends.

After making the stitch, stop before making the final yarn over. Complete the stitch after taking the new yarn. Yarn over using the new yarn and then pull through the remaining loops on the hook. Continue crocheting with the new yarn. After crocheting a few stitches using the new yarn, gently tug the two yarn ends. Make sure to weave in the ends later.

*The Magic Knot*

The magic knot is strong, tiny, and is barely noticeable. There are several ways to make a magic knot. Here, I am going to talk about one way that I feel is easy compared to the others. If you find it uncomfortable, feel free to search for other ways, and choose whatever feels right for you.

Keep crocheting until you are left with just 10 to 12 inches of working yarn. When you are a pro, you won't even need this much yarn. But if you are a beginner, it is better to start off with some extra inches. Lay your new yarn and the working yarn parallel to the working yarn below and the one coming from the left and the one coming from the right, and the new yarn above. Put the working yarn under the new yarn. Then again, bring it over and then across itself. You will have a loop made with the working yarn. Take the working yarn, tie a knot, and pull it tight. Lay the end of the new yarn over the working yarn. Then bring it back under itself and under the working yarn. You will have a loop made of the new yarn. Take the new yarn and tie a knot with it. Pull it tight. Tighten each knot once again to make sure that they are secured. Then take the new yarn in one hand and the working yarn on the other hand. Pull apart. Let the two knots slide together, and then pull tight. Trim the yarn ends carefully as close as possible to the knot. Make sure not to cut the joined yarn or the knot.

*The Russian Join*

It is also a very useful method for joining yarns. It creates a strong, nice join having no ends to weave in. It is going to be a little thick at the join portion, but it is not going to be too noticeable after it gets crocheted.

Take a sharp needle and thread the working yarn onto it. After threading the needle yarn for several inches through the center of the working yarn, gently pull the needle and yarn through. Make sure that there is a loop at the end. Take the new yarn and thread it onto the needle. Then thread it through the loop of the working yarn. Thread the yarn again for several inches through its own piles. Pull the needle and then gently yarn through. Tug on the new yarn and the working yarn for a smooth join. Trim the loose yarn ends carefully.

*The Felted Join*

It is also known as a spit splice. This is because, in this method, you can use your own saliva. You can also use water, and that is what I am going to use while explaining the method. This method is different from animal fiber yarns. The animal fibers yarn has barbs. The moisture and friction make the barbs fuse into one and creates a seamless join. You can use this method on woolen yarns or even on yarns with a little wool of 20%.

You are going to need your yarn and hot or warm water. Then unravel the ends of the new yarn and the working yarn for about three to four inches. Trim the yarn ends (it isn't necessary, but it gives a neat look). This will make sure that the joined area is not way thicker than the rest of the yarn. Trim half of the piles, i.e., if you have four piles, then cut off two piles just where you had unraveled it. Dip the ends in hot water for some time. Take them out of the water and shake off excess moisture. Then place the yarn ends on the palm of your hand in a way that they overlap. Rub your hands. This will felt the yarn. Stop rubbing and then check the strength of the join. Make sure that no ends are sticking out. If so, rub again.

## Fastening Off

After you reach the very end of your crochet design, you will need to fasten off the yarn. "Tie of crochet" and "Fasten of crochet" are the same thing. When you are fastening off a crochet project, you are basically putting a knot in that place so that the crochet doesn't unravel. I will tell you how to fasten off and weave in the ends using a yarn needle securely.

*Step 1*

After finishing working on your last stitch, you will be left with one loop on your hook. Cut the yarn but make sure that you leave a tail of about 15 cm in length. Wrap the yarn around the hook and then pull it through the loop.

*Step 2*

Remove the hook and then pull the tail of the yarn to tighten it up. A nice little knot will be created, which means that your yarn can no longer unravel.

*Step 3*

After you are done fastening off your crochet, you need to do one more thing. You need to hide the yarn tail. Weaving the tail makes it look neat and also secures the tail in place so that the crochet doesn't get unraveled even with a lot of movement. Don't cut the tail right up the fastening off the knot. If you do, it is going to make it loose. For weaving in your ends, take a yarn needle and thread the tail onto it. Weave the needle down, on the wrong side of the crochet, in and out of the back of some stitches.

*Step 4*

Go in an upward direction and weave the needle back. There are no rules as such how to weave in the ends properly, but one important thing that you need to keep in mind is that the ends need to be secured and should not be visible from the front. When the crochet gets pulled, the woven-in tails may come loose sometimes. So, to prevent this from happening, you need to weave the yarn tails in various directions.

# Chapter 4: How to Read a Crochet Pattern?

If you are new to crocheting, trying to read a crochet pattern can seem like reading a foreign language. However, don't let this task of understanding crochet patterns stop you from trying your hand at this incredible craft. You have to learn how to read crochet patterns once you learn the basics of crocheting. A whole new world of crochet will open up for you when you learn how to read crochet patterns. You will be able to improve your skillset and move up beyond just the basics. Some patterns of crocheting are designed aimed at beginners, while some are designed for those who are at a more advanced level.

This chapter aims to help you master the new language of crocheting by helping you read crochet patterns irrespective of whether you are new at crocheting or someone who is just looking for a refresher. There are usually a few similarities between all kinds of crochet patterns. Almost all of them begin with a foundation chain from which you work on all the other stitches. Apart from this, there are also some patterns that begin with a chainless foundation, where you can make your chain and stitches simultaneously and finish the first row.

## Crochet Terms and Abbreviations

Knowing how to read the language of crocheting is one of the main things about understanding any crochet pattern. You need to know the crochet abbreviations before you can start crocheting. The stitches that are used in a crochet pattern are actually written in shorthand, and these are known as crochet abbreviations. This is done because if the full words are written, it could fill up pages and pages. The pattern you are working on will usually come with a chart of abbreviations to indicate what stitches they are using. While you might be able to figure out some of the simpler abbreviations without the help of a guide, it might take you some time to remember the others.

Following is a list of abbreviations used in creating crochet patterns:

- **APPROX** – Approximately
- **ALT** – Alternate
- **BO** – Bobble
- **BL or BLO** – Back loop or back loop only
- **BET** – Between
- **BEG** – Begin or beginning
- **BP** – Back post
- **BPTR** – Back post treble crochet
- **BPSC** – Back post single crochet
- **BPHDC** – Back post half double crochet
- **BPDTR** – Back post double treble crochet
- **BPDC** – Back post double crochet
- **CONT** – Continue
- **CL** – Cluster
- **CH** – Chain stitch
- **CC** – Contrasting color

- **CH-SP** – Chain space

- **DEC** – Decrease

- **DC** – Double crochet

- **DTR** – Double treble crochet

- **DC2TOG** – Double crochet two stitches together

- **ETR** – Extended treble crochet

- **ESC** – Extended single crochet

- **EHDC** – Extended half double crochet

- **EDC** – Extended double crochet

- **FOLL** – Following

- **FL/FLO** – Front loop/front loop only

- **FP** – Front post

- **FPSC** – Front post single crochet

- **FPHDC** – Front post half double crochet

- **FPDTR** – Front post double treble crochet

- **FPDC** – Front post double crochet

- **YOH** – Yarn over hook

- **YO** – Yarn over

- **WS** – Wrong side

# Common Terms and Measurements

- ( ) – work a group of stitches all in a single space or stitch or apply the instructions given within the parenthesis the given number of times

- [ ] – Work out the instructions given within the brackets the given number of times

- { } – Work out the instructions provided within the brackets the given number of times

- * - The instructions given after a single asterisk are to be repeated as many times as directed

- ** - The instructions written between asterisks are to be repeated at specific locations or as many times as directed

# Reading Crochet Patterns

Here is a basic guide that could help you in reading crochet patterns:

- **See the name of the crochet pattern** – Even though it might appear very obvious, the first step to determining whether you want to try a particular crochet pattern is by reading its title. You will get to know whether the pattern is for a blanket or a scarf, or something else. The title might also provide you some idea about the difficulty of the pattern.

- **Check the difficulty of the pattern** – The difficulty of a particular crochet pattern is generally given under its title. Study the pattern and try to determine whether it's made for beginner, intermediate, or advanced-level crocheters. If you are only a beginner trying to learn how to crochet, there is no reason for you to try to understand a crochet pattern designed for advanced-level crocheters.

- **Figure out the size of the finished project** — Try to figure out the finished measurements of the project. If the crochet pattern is for something wearable, the available sizes for it will be given.

- **Check the list of materials** — The crochet pattern you have chosen will tell you what the weight of the yarn should be and the kind of yarn that you can use. You will also get to know about the amount of yarn that's required to finish the project. The crochet pattern will also tell you if there are any other materials that are required and even about the size of the crochet you need to purchase.

- **Read the crochet abbreviations and terms** — Some of the most commonly used crochet abbreviations and terms are already listed above. You can easily understand what you have to perform if you know the abbreviations, terms, and symbols. For example, a pattern might say:

Row 1: Ch 12; sc in 3rd third ch from hook and in every ch across. This tells you to create twelve chain stitches loosely after making a slip knot on the hook. Then, skip the first chain and make single crochet in the third chain away from the hook.

- **Understanding crochet tensions** — Also known as a gauge, it is the quantity of fabric that a particular kind of yarn and a particular hook size will create. You can check your gauge by crocheting a swatch that's four by four inches in the stitch pattern that is given in the crochet instructions. Try a larger hook if your gauge is smaller than that listed in the pattern. Try a smaller hook if it's larger. Understanding the gauge or crochet tension is crucial if you want to create something that has to be true to size.

# Chapter 5: 25 Patterns That You Should Know

In Chapter 3, I have explained some basic stitches that you should know. Once you master that, it's time to move on to the different important patterns that are there. With these stitches, there are a lot of fun projects that you can do. They are not only enjoyable but also quite easy. Yes, if you are a beginner, you will need practice, but after a while, you can complete even the most intricate projects in no time.

I have made these tutorials with the most basic steps so that it's easy to understand for you. There are some common abbreviations used, and I hope you have learned them in Chapter 4. Once you are comfortable with these, you can move on to more ambitious projects.

## Pineapple Lace

If you look at the vintage crocheted laces, then you will find the pineapple lace over there very frequently. Once you learn the pattern, you will be able to recognize it in a lot of places, and you can also use this pattern in a lot of beautiful designs. When you see this pattern, you might think that this is a complicated one, but in reality, it is quite easy to make.

The pineapple crochet is not just of one type, but there are variations as well. Here, in this section, I am going to teach you the steps that will help you make a pineapple motif of your own. But the more you brush up on your skills, the more you will realize that the pineapple lace can be tried in different ways.

Every time you hear someone talking about the pineapple lace stitch, they are, in all probability, talking about the type of lace that I am going to teach here. But the pineapple stitch is also present in the form of an antique stitch pattern that many people know of. You can make the pineapple lace designs in various sizes, and you can use both yarn or thread as per your preference. You can either stitch different pineapples together to form a crochet pattern, or you can also use them one at a time on doilies or appliques. Learning this motif will take you one step closer to mastering the different patterns that have the pineapple lace in it.

The pattern that I have included here is the basic one that you will get everywhere. In some places, you might get some slight modifications, but this is the base you need. You can make skirts, shawls, and even tablecloths after learning this pattern.

**Step 1** – Let's begin with the first step. Like most other patterns, this one also starts with a chain and a very short one. The motif's base will be formed by this chain. So, first, you have to chain 4.

**Step 2** – Take the foundation chain that you just made and work your first row into it. Count the 4th chain starting from the hook and make all the stitches in that chain.

Make one dc (double crochet). Chain 2. Crochet two double crochet.

The first dc is formed by the starting chain, so if you see it in that way, then you have a row of two double crochet, chain two, two double crochet. Your pineapple motif's base has been formed.

**Step 3** – Now, first, you have to turn the work. From the previous row, count the chain two space and in that space, make 13 tr (treble crochet) stitches. Here is a simpler breakdown of this step –

Turn. Your first tr is when you chain 4. Crochet 12 treble crochets into chain two.

**Step 4** – You have to turn the work again and then chain four. When you make this chain, it will be counted as the first tr.

After this, chain 1, and then make one treble crochet into each tr across. So, if you continue it this way, the first treble that you made in the previous row should be where your last treble of this step ends.

When this step is over, count the number of tr stitches you have that are separated by chain one spaces, and the number must be 13.

**Step 5** – Now, there are a bunch of stitches that you will be working on – there will be chains and single crochets. In fact, this is also what the rest of the motif looks like.

First, turn the work that you have done—chain 3.

In the first chain-one space, make a single crochet.

Repeat the process (ch 3, sc) throughout the row. Every chain-one space in that row has to be worked into.

When you finish, you will have a total of twelve chain-three spaces.

**Step 6** – In this step, too, it will seem as if you are repeating everything you did in Step 5, but there is one thing that is different. Every time, the 1st chain-three space will be skipped.

Start by turning the work. Then, skip the first chain-three space.

Chain 3, then make one single crochet in the next chain-three space.

Repeat the process (chain 3, sc in next chain-3 space). The same thing will be done across the entire row.

When you finish this step, you will have a row of eleven chain-3 spaces.

**Step 7** – Here, you will keep repeating what you learned in Step 6. But every row will have one chain-three space less. This is because the first chain-3 space is being skipped every time. Continue doing this until there is only one chain-3 space remaining at the top. Here your pineapple motif ends.

Weave off the ends.

## Loop Stitch

There is no abbreviation for the loop stitch. But do you about the story behind the naming of this stitch? Well, when you finish this stitch, you will notice that there are long loops that are somewhat loose are left behind, and that is what gives this stitch its name. It will require some time, patience, and practice on your part to keep all these loops of the same length. But with time, you are soon going to get the hang of it, and you will see how every garment is amped up with this simple pattern.

This is quite a fun little trick, but at first, I must warn you, it might seem a bit awkward to you. You simply need to get into the flow to master this one. This stitch can be varied in a lot of different ways. If you want the final outcome to be a bit fuzzier, then you can even choose to cut the loops. And if you want the design to be flashy, then you can also put a bead in every loop. Now, let's get started with the steps.

**Step 1** – Take your yarn hand and then wrap the yarn on your index finger from front to back. In this step, most people are concerned about what the length of the loop should be. Well, it depends on how tight or loose you want the wrap to be.

**Step 2** – In the next stitch, you have to insert the hook. This will ensure that on your hook, you have two loops. Now, from behind the index finger, grab the yarn, and then insert the yarn into the stitch and draw it from the other side. The loop will form with the help of the yarn on your finger.

**Step 3** — Now, you take the loop on your index finger; you will have to draw the yarn through the two loops on the hook after you yarn over the hook. If you want the finished look to be perfect, you have to ensure that all the loops have the same size. And if you want the shaggy look, cut all the loops after you have finished.

**Step 4** — In order to get a row of loops like these, repeat the process.

## Brick Stitch

This is another vintage stitch pattern that you are going to learn in this chapter. This pattern is known by a variety of different names, some of which are the crazy shell and the crazy stitch. But whatever the name is, the stitch definitely looks beautiful and attractive and is also a fun one to learn. The stitches used here are totally basic, and so, even if you are a beginner, you should have no problem learning this one.

If you have seen a diagonal box stitch, then you might confuse it with the brick stitch because they look somewhat similar. Without any further ado, let's have a look at how you can crochet this pattern.

**Step 1** — So, first, you need a foundation chain to make this pattern. The chain that you make has to be a multiple of 3 + 1. Let us say you want the chain to be three times of 6 + 1; then your starting chain has to be 19. After that, follow the rest of the instructions.

From the hook, count the fourth chain, and in it, make three double crochets.

*Then, skip three stitches. Make a single crochet in the next chain. After that, chain three. Make three double crochet in the same chain.*

Now, all the way across the row, you have to repeat the steps mentioned with the asterisk. In the last chain, make a single crochet.

**Step 2** – Now, we start the next row. This also applies to all the subsequent rows that are to follow. The same pattern will be followed.

Turn the work and chain three.

In the previous row, the single crochet where you ended will now have three double crochet in it.

*In the next chain-3 space, make a single crochet. After that, chain three. In the same chain-3 space, make three double crochet.*

Work across the row and repeat the steps mentioned within the asterisk, and in this way, you will reach the last chain-3 space. The final chain-3 space will not have the same pattern.

In the final chain-3 space, make one single crochet.

**Step 3** – Every additional row you make will have the same set of instructions, as mentioned in Step 2.

Once you get the hang of this pattern, you will see how easy it is. When you finish the pattern, you will be able to see how the individual boxes that are formed look like bricks and hence, the name.

## Bullion Stitch

If you have seen a bullion stitch before, then you'll know that they have this distinctly puffy look about them that sets them apart from other stitches. Their puffiness also adds texture to the project you are working on. But many crocheters think that the bullion stitch is a medium-level pattern. However, I assure you that it is much easier than it looks, and I have described it in very easy steps. All you need is your crochet hook, the yarn of your choice, and some basic knowledge of the stitches, and you are good to go. So, let us see what are the steps. As you move on, you'll notice that it is quite a neat technique.

**Step 1** – You need the foundation row to begin a bullion stitch and for that, make a chain of fifteen stitches. You can alter the number of stitches here, depending on the project that you are doing. Then, make your first row by making single crochets throughout until the very end of the chain.

**Step 2** – Once you have created the first row and you have reached the end, chain two. After that, turn all the stitches around. This is what is known as the turning chain, and you have to do this every time you are going to start a new row.

**Step 3** – Now, in order to do this stitch, you have to wrap the yarn around the hook but not once; you have to loop it seven times. Make sure the yarn is not overlapping, but it should be close. In case you want your stitch to be larger, you can increase the number of loops on the hook, but for practice, this should be enough.

**Step 4** – Find the next stitch in the row, insert the hook into it, and yarn over. When you pull the yarn through, pull it through the next loop on the hook.

**Step 5** – Wrap the yarn over the hook again, and in this way, keep pulling the yarn through all the loops. You don't have to do it at once. Instead, do it one at a time. Once you have pulled it through all the loops, you have officially completed your first bullion stitch.

**Step 6** – Now, if you want the second round of bullion stitches, you first have to make another row of single crochets to work into and then follow the rest of the steps as mentioned above.

**Step 7** – When all your stitches are over, make sure you leave a tail before snipping a yarn. Tugging at this tail will give you a tighter knot. If you want it to stay secure, you can even knot it, and any excess yarn can then be snipped.

## Spiral Stitch

The process involved in carrying out a spiral crochet stitch is not very different from a regular crochet stitch made in the round, but it still has a starkly different design as well as impact. A spiral stitch is actually a very rare pattern to see in crochet designs, and it is indeed a treat to your eyes, owing to its interesting color schemes, which cause an illusion for the viewer's eyes.

There are quite a few different ways to do a multi-color spiral stitch. One of the easiest and common ways which are practiced is the basic two-color spiral crochet, the steps to which are as follow:

**Step 1** – Start with color 1, and use ten half double crochet stitches in total. Make two different chains- one with 9 half double crochets, and the other with 1. Remember to not use a slip stitch at the end of a round.

**Step 2** – Now, you can change colors and switch over to color 2. You can either keep switching between the two colors which are being used, or you can finish each round by fastening them off as you proceed by continuing to carry the yarn up to the back of the motif that you are making. This step will be using 20 half double crochet stitches in total.

**Step 3** – In this step, you have to switch back to the first color which you used earlier, in Step 1. Without using a slip stitch, work your way all around the design using half double crochets, having a total of 30 of them to finish this step off.

**Step 4** – Repeat the procedure mentioned in Step 2, except switch to the second color being used this time. Keep in mind that by the end of this step, the total number of half double crochet stitches being used should be 40.

These are the four steps essential to a basic two-color spiral stitch. Now, as the pattern keeps expanding, the color shifts, making the design of the spiral more prominent and eye-catching; however, the overall appearance will still be somewhat subtle compared to the two-color spiral crochet pattern with a mid-round color change (which guarantees more vibrant results), steps to which are given below:

**Step 1** – Start with the first color, and make four double crochets in the first chain. Next, shift to the second color and carry out the same process.

**Step 2** – Carry on with the second color, making two double crochets on the top of the first chain and to each of the next four stitches. Change colors, and make two double crochets to the next five stitches.

**Step 3** – Keep working with the first color, making one double-cross to the first chain and 2 to the second chain. Repeat the process five times, then switch to the next color and carry out the entire procedure with that in the same way.

**Step 4** – Begins with the second color and switch back to the first one, repeating the procedure mentioned above in Step 4, until you have made a total of 40 double crochets.

## Basket Weave

Basketweave crochet stands apart because of its beautiful texture, and this pattern is quite easy to make if you are a little familiar with post stitches. Basketweave crochets has several uses, the most common of them being a baby blanket, as this pattern makes sure to produce something which is warm and cozy while ensuring that there are no holes in between the stitches into which the baby's toes or fingers might get caught up, therefore making it really convenient as well.

The equipment you will need to make a basket weave includes one crochet hook, one novelty yarn, and three bulky-weave yarns of different colors each. Before starting, decide on the blanket size you are making. Even if you do not have the specifics, get an approximate idea about the exact dimensions of the end product, you are envisioning. Next, follow these steps to carry this crochet stitch out efficiently:

**Step 1** – Start with crocheting a foundation chain that is a little shorter than the width of your blanket. The foundation row must have enough chains which can accommodate your choice. Which means, if you want to make five crochets per stitch, you need to make sure that the foundation row has a multiple of five, added to the number required for your turning chain.

**Step 2** – Work on the first row, and crochet your choice of stitch into each stitch across. If you are using a double crochet stitch (which is one of the most used crochets for the basketweave), make one double crochet for every single stitch present across the row.

**Step 3** – Next, move on to the post stitches, starting with your turning chain. Work on alternating back and front post double cross stitches and do this across the entire row in groups.

**Step 4** – In the next step, you will move on to crocheting the next group of rows. Each of these rows will be alternating between a front post double crochet and a back post double crochet to make sure that the aligning stitches are always protruding out from the same side.

**Step 5** – Once one set of rows have been completed, you need to reverse the direction. For this, crochet in the exact opposite way (front for back, and vice-versa). This way, the texture of your post stitches will now be protruding in a similar manner, but from the direction opposite to the one, which is the result of the process mentioned above in Step 4.

**Step 6** – Once you are done with crocheting the first new row (in the opposite direction), go back to before, working in a way that you continue alternating front posts into back posts and the other way round. Continue working on the row, switching your direction every few rows (the number for this should be five if you are following this pattern, and anywhere between 3 and 7 in general) until you finish the product that you have been working on.

## Thick and Thin Front Loop Single Crochet

This stitch is mostly for beginners as it employs basic stitches. It makes use of only the front loop single crochet stitch, which is a variation of the single crochet. The thick and thin front loop single crochet can create various textures, which is slightly lacy. The best way to get the perfect result is to use different yarn sizes. As this stitch is mostly worked in rows, so it's not important for you to know how to create round or joint motifs. At the same time, each row will be equal in length, so it is also not necessary to know how to decrease or increase the crochet in order to complete your work. This method, for its unique texture, is used to create various original and eye-catching designs in scarfs mostly and also shawls.

Thick and thin front loop single crochet, as the name suggests, creates a mixture of thick and thin sections in the pattern you are working on, giving it a texture that is mostly bulky but extremely cozy. And if you create a blocked pattern, the overall effect is mostly lacy.

**Step 1** – When you are working on the first row, use a heavier yarn and crochet the base or the foundation chain. Now keep in mind that you need to work on the entire row by creating only single crochet stitches.

**Step 2** – For the second row, start working on the entire row by using the front loop single crochet stitch, which is extremely similar to the single crochet stitch, with only the difference being that you need to work through the front loops only. You have to keep another thing in mind that before you finish the last step of this last stitch in this row, you need to change to the lesser weight yarn.

**Step 3** – After this, when you are working on your third and fourth row, use the yarn to create two more rows of the front loop single crochet stitch. Before you finish the last step of this last stitch, you need to change to the heavyweight yarn.

Keep in mind that you need to constantly change between the lighter and the heavier thread for two rows. Create two rows with lighter thread and two rows with heavier thread. Continue these steps.

There are few tips for you to create a successful pattern using the thick and thin front loop single crochet. Please keep in mind that you should never change the crochet hook you are using when you are switching one type of yarn to another. Always use the same crochet hook throughout the pattern. It is better to choose such a hook, which will let you be comfortable when you stitch both the lighter and heavier yarn.

It is a common mistake to tighten your tension as you are working with the lightweight thread. But this is a mistake you should not make as that will destroy the beauty of your pattern. Always maintain a loose tension on your threads as you don't want your pattern to get distorted.

## Granite Stitch

Granite stitch is also known as the crochet moss stitch. This is quite an easy stitching technique, and you can easily ace it if you are familiar with two basic stitches, which are the single crochet stitch and the chain stitch. Some easy projects which you might want to work on using the granite, or the crochet moss stitch, include a baby blanket, a scarf, beanie, or even a headband. All of these are projects you can easily work on using the procedure mentioned here, and it is also a good way of settling into the stitching method before you start working on a little more complicated projects.

To get you started, here are a few easy-to-follow steps for how to go about a granite stitch:

**Step 1** – Begin with putting together a foundation chain. Make sure the foundation has an odd number of chains in it, as the crochet stitch would not really work otherwise.

**Step 2** – For the first row in the foundation chain, place a marker in the first chain from the hook. Next, in the third chain from your hook, make a single crochet. Put another chain stitch after that, skip the next chain, and then make another single crochet stitch in the chain after that. Repeat this entire process all throughout the row. To end this process, make a final chain stitch, and then turn the hook.

**Step 3** – For the second row, repeat the sequence – a single crochet stitch in the next chain, followed by a chain stitch- across the entire row. Once you are done with the procedure, at the very end of the row, make a single crochet stitch, and make sure this point is where you had placed your marker earlier (as mentioned in step 2). Before working on this stitch, you can consider removing the marker. Once the stitch is done, make a chain stitch, and turn the hook.

**Step 4** – For the third row and the remaining rows which follow it (depending on the number of chains you had chosen for your foundation), work them in the same way as you had stitched the second row (following the procedure mentioned in step 3). Except, this time, you need to do one thing differently- once you are done with working the row, work the last single crochet stitch into a turning chain for the previous row. Make sure to repeat the complete row for as long as it takes to make sure that the piece you are working on is of the perfect length which you were aiming for.

Once you have gotten used to the stitch, you do not need to guide yourself by placing the marker at the end of the chains any longer. It is just an easy trick to aid your stitching, and the process can be carried on in just the same way without the marker as well, and it is more convenient if you do now have to place and remove the marker constantly.

## Puff Stitch

A puff stitch is one of the slightly more complicated crochet stitching techniques. It is basically a variation of the half double crochet technique. There are different variations of the puff stitch, and these variations usually depend on the number of loops used as well as the size of the puff stitch. Some other types of puff stitches include staggered puff stitches, zigzag stitches, stacked, braided, and so on. A puff stitch helps you form fluffy and thick bobbles with double sides. These bobbles can then be utilized to form smaller motifs. The equipment you will need to make a puff stitch is simply a yarn and a crochet hook. Figuring out the tension needed to perfect the puff stitch will take you some practice, but here are some helpful tips and tricks on how to get started with the basics of it:

**Step 1** – Begin with creating a foundation – or starting a chain. Make sure your starting chain is made in the multiples of two stitches plus four. To make a stitch that is more effective, you can consider working with a yarn that is not easily prone to splitting and a hook that matches with the size recommended on the label of the yarn.

**Step 2** – Next, you will need to insert your hook in the fourth chain. First, wrap the yarn over the hook, and then insert the hook into the fourth chain (if you count from the starting point of the hook). Follow it by yarning over again and then drawing it into a loop. This way, you should have at least three loops on the hook that you are using. This would be the starting point for a half double crochet stitch.

**Step 3** – In this step, you will need to put your hook in through the same chain stitch. Cross the yarn over, and then draw it over another loop. At this point, you should be having five loops on your hook (if you had three on your hook in the last step).

**Step 4** – Repeat the entire procedure mentioned in step 3. Do this until you have the exact number of loops on your hook, which is needed for the puff stitch that you are aiming to create. While some puff stitches are complete with as few as just five stitched over the hook, some other variations of this crocheting technique will require you to have nine to eleven loops. Make sure that you are clear about the details of the stitch before starting so that it is easy to follow through.

**Step 5** – Once you have the required number of loops on the hook, yarn over and draw the yarn through all of your loops. Make sure that the hook is steady, and there is as little wiggling as needed so that the loops are not pulled from their positions.

**Step 6** – In this final step, you will need to secure the puff stitch with a chain. Once the loops are in place, make a single chain stitch. This will secure the entire puff stitch and help keep it upright.

**Step 7** – When you are working across rows, you will have to skip a chain and then work a puff stitch (in the same way mentioned above) into the next row. Repeal the procedure with all your rows. At the end of each row, flip your yarn and create a turning chain using three chain stitches.

## Basic Crochet V Stitch

One among those knots is known as the V-stitch, which is actually pretty simple and doesn't take much time. It's usually used when taking up huge crocheting projects like making *afghans*.

**Step 1** – Start by making the foundation chain and the first row. Use the yarn to create double crochet into the fourth stitch from your hook. The first three chains in the row are counted as a double crochet. Now you have the equivalent of two double crochet stitches at the starting of the row, giving your work a nice edge.

**Step 2** – Now skip the next chain and start working on another double crochet stitch into your next chain stitch. This forms the first part of your V-stitch. Finish this and work another double crochet stitch into the same stitch where last worked on to complete your V-stitch.

**Step 3** – You have to start making the next V-stitch now by yarning over the hook to start the first double crochet into the V-stitch. Then you will need to skip the next two chain stitches. You will have chain 1 of your double crochet then. The V-stitch is completed by this double crochet in the same chain stitch.

You will then need to repeat these steps and work on a given pattern. As you reach the end of the row, create a chain stitch followed by filling up the last two stitches with one double crochet stitch each.

**Step 4** – Now, you need to create three chain stitches for making the turning chain. Turn your yarned pattern over to start crocheting the second row by working back across the first row.

**Step 5** – After this, you need to begin the second row of V-stitch. The turning chain that you just created will be counted as your first double crochet stitch. You need to fill up your next double crochet with a double crochet stitch now.

**Step 6** – You will now need to place the hook for the first V-stitch in the row. Each V-stitch you are starting will have to be worked into the middle of the V-stitch that you have stitched in the row below. (Note- while making a V-stitch, place the hook in the space available between the V and not into the chain stitch.)

**Step 7** – Next, in the chain one region below, you need to double crochet in the V-stitch. In order to complete the V-stitch, create another double crochet. Finally, to create any pattern using this stitch, continue working one V-stitch into each V-stitch across the row. Then end the row as before.

## Basic Shell Stitch

The basic shell stitch is an advanced beginner's stitch to add a decorative appeal to any crocheting project. It can be used to make the border and the rows as well.

**Step 1** – Make your starting chain in order to begin row 1. First, start with your foundation chain. It should consist of a series of chain stitches in a pattern of six stitches plus one. To give an example, when you are starting a chain, start with, say, 31, which has five multiples of six and one extra stitch. Now, you need to work one single crochet stitch into the second stitch from your hook.

**Step 2** – Now, firstly skip the next two chain stitches, and then you need to create a double crochet stitch into your next chain stitch after that. This should be followed by you working four double stitches into that same chain stitch because you need a total of five double crochet stitches. This creates the shell stitch.

**Step 3** – In order to anchor the first crochet shell, you need to skip the next two chain stitches. After that, start working a single crochet stitch into your next chain stitch immediately after the unworked chains. Congratulation! You now have your first anchored shell stitch complete.

**Step 4** – You will have to repeat the following process now – you will need to skip the next two chains, followed by working five double crochet stitches in your next chin stitch. Create one single crochet in the next chain. Keep on repeating this until you come to the end of the row, where you need to end the line with single crochet in your final stitch.

**Step 5** – This step is for those who want to experiment with colors. After you work the last crochet at the end of the row, attach the new colored yarn and then complete the stitch. Now, create a turning chain comprising of three chain stitches. This is your first double crochet stitch in your new row.

When you are working with more than one color, it is always advisable to weave in the ends as you are stitching. What you need to do is, cut the first color and then weave in the end along with that end, which was created at the starting of your work. You could also crochet the ends in order to secure them.

**Step 6** – You will have to begin your second row with a half shell. Turn your pattern around and create two double crochet stitches into your first stitch. If you have already counted your turning chain as your double crochet stitch, then this will give you a total of three stitches at the starting of the row.

After this, you need to skip two stitches and create a single crochet stitch into your next double crochet. Work into the center stitch in the grouping of the shell stitches in the row below.

**Step 7** – As you continue the second row, skip two stitches, and create a group of five double crochets into your next stitch. As you reach the end of the row, create the last crochet stitch into your turning stitch.

Repeat this technique until you reach your desired length of the work.

# Crocodile Stitch

As the name suggests, the crocodile stitch looks like the scales of a reptile or like the feathers of a bird when completed. Due to the unique style that is employed in creating it, first, a row of foundation double crochet stitches is made, followed by double crochet stitches that look like the scales. This stitch will look fantastic if used to make costumes that have the essence of fantasy to it.

**Step 1** – You have to start working on the foundation row at first. Chain a multiple of 6+3 chain stitches. For example, create a chain of 33 stitches. These three chains form your first double crochet. Now very carefully, work a double crochet into your third chain from the hook. Keep in mind that you need to chain two and skip two chains after this. After this, work two double crochet stitches into your next chain. You will need to repeat this till the end of the row.

End with a set of two double crochet stitches. This forms the foundation of the first row of crocodile stitches. Next, you have to create scales onto your double crochet 'posts' from this row.

**Step 2** – Keep the foundation row to your right and create chain 3. This is your first double crochet. You have to now create four such double crochets on the first post of your foundation row.

Place the foundation row on your left now. Create five double crochet stitches on the second post of your foundation row.

Now place the top of your foundation row on your right. You need to skip the next few posts, which are obscured by the first scale. Go on to work five double crochets into the first double crochet of the next set of posts. After pivoting the foundation row, create five double crochets into your second double crochet of this set of posts.

Repeat the above-mentioned process across the row as you create a crocodile stitch on every other set of posts.

**Step 3** – After completing this first row, create the next foundation row consisting of double crochet posts and chain stitch spaces. Work a chain three as this will create your first double crochet. Then take your last crocodile stitch and create one double crochet into its center.

Now create two double crochets in between the two crocodile stitches as you work your way between two double crochets from your first foundation row. You have your chain two now. Create two double crochets in the center of your next crocodile stitch. Now repeat this chain two till the end of the row.

**Step 4** – You will need to create each scale on the set of posts between these scales from the first row so that on your right, you have the top. In chain one, skip the first set of double crochet and create five double crochet on the 1st double crochet of the next posts. After pivoting the foundation row, create five double crochets on the 2nd double crochet. Repeat this.

At the end of the row, slip stitch between the two posts. You have chain three now, which is the first double crochet. Then take the previous row and double crochet between the two posts. Take chain two and create two double crochets into the center of the next crocodile stitch.

Continue adding further rows of foundation double crochets till you reach your desired length.

## Suzette Stitch

Once you have learned the basics, this stitch should seem pretty easy to you. This is a sturdy pattern and is formed of both double and single crochets. But the best thing about this pattern is that it is a reversible one, and so it can be used in a variety of projects like washcloths, blankets, and so on. Here is how you can make this stitch.

**Step 1** – Make your starting chain. Chain 22.

**Step 2** – First, you have to make a single crochet and then a double. So, count the second chain starting from the hook and make single crochet in it. In the same chain, make a double crochet.

**Step 3** – Now, you have to skip one chain. In the next chain, make a single crochet. Again, like Step 2, make a double crochet in the same chain.

**Step 4** – Follow the same process as in Step 3 across the row, skip a chain, and then in the next stitch, make a single and double crochet. After that, in the last chain, make one single crochet. Now, the 1st row of the Suzette stitch is complete.

**Step 5** – Chain and then turn the piece. In the 1st stitch of the row, make one single crochet. In the same stitch, make a double crochet.

**Step 6** – Now, skip one stitch. To help you identify better, the stitch that you will be skipping here is the double crochet that you did in the previous row. In the next stitch, make one single crochet followed by one double crochet.

**Step 7** – The previous step will have to be repeated all along the row until you have only two stitches. The next stitches will have to be skipped until you reach the last stitch, where you will make one single crochet.

**Step 8** – To continue with the pattern, you simply have to keep repeating the 2nd row over and over again. The rhythm will set in your hands when you become habituated with the pattern.

## Lemon Peel Stitch

Thi stitch is also one of the basic crochet stitches that you can make use of in a variety of projects. It can be used in kitchen accessories, garments, and even blankets. The texture that you get from this stitch somewhat feels like an actual lemon and hence, the name. The bumpy feel of the project comes from the fact that you are alternating the stitches. In general, you can call it a bumpy stitch, but with the right hook and yarn combination, you can actually bring a nice drape to it. Here are the steps for making this stitch.

**Step 1** – First, you need a starting chain. The number of stitches can be anything depending on your preference, but if you have an even number of chains, then it will be easier to work for you. So, you need a basic starting chain first.

**Step 2** – As a turning chain, chain one. Coun the second chain from the hook, and make one single crochet in it.

**Step 3** – In the next stitch, make a double crochet.

**Step 4** –Step 2 and 3 will have to be repeated all across the row. First, you have to make a single crochet stitch, and then, you have to make a double crochet stitch. If you continue doing this, then your row should end in a double crochet stitch.

**Step 5** – Now, you have to work on the next row. Start by turning the chain and repeat all the steps.

So, every time you think about crocheting a pattern that is simple yet not basic, the lemon peel stitch is what you need.

## An Infinity Scarf

An infinity scarf is a continuous circle of fabric yarned through crocheting instead of being one long rectangle fabric. As the name suggests, it doesn't have a beginning or end. It's very easy to learn, and if you are just starting out with crocheting, you shouldn't have any problem making one. Choose a hook from 1-9 size and a tapestry needle.

**Step 1** – How long your scarf will be will depend upon the length of the chain you are starting with. To make the necessary adjustments to your scarf, create the chain with as many stitches that can be divided by 4 and 6. Slip stitch to join together the ends of the chain to the starting, and try to be careful to keep your chain straight. Don't let it twist.

**Step 2** – On your chain one, create one single crochet in each of your chains around for the total length you want to create, say 288 single crochets. Slip stitch in order to join your work to the first single crochet slip stitch in the round.

Next, take chain 3. This is your first double crochet in the round. Double crochet in your next stitch. (As for chain 2, skip the next two chains and create one double crochet in every next two double crochet)

Repeat this. Now, slip stitch to join the end of the round with the beginning. You will then have a total of 114 double crochet stitches and 57 chain stitch spaces in that particular round.

**Step 3** – On your chain one, create one single crochet in every double crochet and two single crochets in every chain-two space. Now slip stitch to join the beginning to the end. You will now have 288 single crochet stitches in your round.

Your chain 3 is your one half double crochets plus one chain. You will have to skip the next stitch. Repeat this sequence. Slip stitch your work to attach it with the 2nd chain stitch in the round. You will now have a total of 114 half double crochets and 114 chain-one space in that round.

**Step 4** – After this, slip stitch in the next chain-two space, chain 3. This is your one half double crochet. Repeat this. Then, slip stitch to attach to the 2nd chain stitch in the round.

Repeat the above step. You could change the length of the scarf if you want by either omitting few rows or adding a few.

**Step 5** – Next, you need to slip stitch in the next chain-two space. Then create single crochet in chain one and single crochet in the next half double crochet.

Repeat this. After this, repeat step two, as mentioned above.

Lastly, in order to form the edging, begin the crochet hook inside the active loop. Skip the next two stitches. Then repeat this sequence in the brackets all around. You should ideally get 38 crochet shells. As you complete working the round of shell stitches, create a round of surface crochet slip stitches in the spot where the last round touches the shell stitch edging round.

Repeat this on the other side as you work back across the free loops in the starting chain.

## Classic Granny Square

A classic granny square is one of the most basic and easy to master designs that you learn in your initial days of crocheting. Once you get a fair idea, you can expand upon that design to suit your needs, from blankets to bags to placement decors. You will need a size H crochet hook and one skein of worsted-weight yarn.

A classic granny square is created in the round by using double crochet stitches made in clusters of three with two chain stitches used to separate the sets.

**Step 1** – Though there are many ways to start a granny square, yet we recommend starting with a slip knot. Next, chain three. This is your first double crochet stitch first cluster.

**Step 2** – To complete this, create two double crochets in your base chain of chain3. You will now have three double stitches next to one another in the first group. Now, chain two.

**Step 3** – You will need to create another cluster of three double crochets into the base of the first chain 3 round. (this is the same place where you had made the other double crochet stitch from the previous group that you had created). Chain two.

**Step 4** – Repeat the above-mentioned step twice after this. You now have four clusters of double crochets that have chain-two space between them, and the last two should be hanging on the end.

In order to close this round and work on the square shape, you will have to slip stitch on the top of your first chain 3. Your first round ends here.

**Step 5** – You will have to start round two with chain three again. This will be your first double crochet of the first set.

**Step 6** – After this, create two double crochets next to chain 3 in the corner that is open immediately below your chain 3. With the first double crochet cluster, your chain two is finished.

**Step 7** – Next, you will have to crochet three double crochets in the corner, then chain two, and create another three double crochets in the same place in the corner. You will need to work all the corners this way, except for the starting corner.

**Step 8** – As you reach the corner, you started from, create another cluster of 3 double crochets, then chain 2. After this, slip stitch to the top of the first chain 3 to close the round. All the corners should now look the same.

**Step 9** – Begin the third round as you did with the previous rounds. Chain three, and in that space, create two double crochets—chain 2.

**Step 10** – Then, you will have to crochet a cluster of 3 double crochets in the place on the side of the square and then chain 2.

**Step 11** – Once again, work the corners as you have done previously. Make a cluster consisting of three double crochets on each corner, chain two, and then another cluster and chain two.

Repeat the previous steps as you go around, so you should get a cluster on every side and two clusters in each corner.

Lastly, as you reach the final corner, create a cluster of double crochets, chain two, and then slip stitch to close the round.

Finish your granny square by cutting the thread, leaving a tail of 6 inches, and then weave in the ends.

## Snowflake

It's winter now, and guess what that means? Holidays are here, and you need to be prepared with your home décor ideas. Crochet snowflakes are a beautiful choice when you want your house to look beautiful, and they are very easy to make. You will need a 3.5 mm crochet hook, a blocking mat, or towels and pins. Use cotton fingering weight yarn and any kind of stiffening solution. The size of your snowflake will slightly depend on the size of the yarn you are using.

It can be very easily made with the basic stitches you know with just another new stitch that you will have to learn, that is the treble or the triple crochet. However, you will need to work several stitch patterns and shapes into the same stitch many times. So, make sure to follow the instructions carefully.

**Step 1** – Start with making a slip knot and chain six. Join this using a slip stitch to make a ring.

**Step 2** – To create the foundation, create chain two that will count as 1st single crochet plus chain-one space. *Single crochet into the ring and then chain 1*. Perform the step between the asterisk five times and then slip stitch to the first chain in order to join, and you will have a total of 12 stitches.

**Step 3** – Next, you need to create a puff stitch three times, yarn over your hook, and then pull the yarn through all the seven loops.

Then, chain 1 to complete your puff stitch.

Then, make four chain stitches, and *puff stitch in chain-one space, chain 1, double crochet in next stitch, chain 1* repeat this step within asterisk five times. Then, make a puff stitch in the chain-one space, chain one. In the first stitch, find the third chain, and join to it with the help of a slip stitch.

**Step 4** – Now, to create your snowflake branches, slip stitch in your chain-one space.

*In chain-one stitch that closes the puff stitch, make the following [(double crochet, chain one, treble crochet); chain three, in the third chain from the hook, make a slip stitch; (treble crochet, chain one, double crochet)], then skip one stitch. In the next double crochet, make the following stitches [slip stitch, (chain seven, slip stitches in the 5th, then 6th, then 7th chains from the hook    ), slip stitch], now, skip two stitches* repeat the steps within the asterisk four times.

Then, in the chain-one space that closes the puff stitch, make the following stitches [(double crochet, chain one, treble crochet), chain three, from the hook, count the third chain and make a slip stitch in it; (treble crochet, chain 1, double crochet)], then skip a stitch. Now, at the end of the previous round, find the slip stitch and at the top of it make these stitches [slip stitch, (chain seven, slip stitch in 5th, then 6th, then 7th chain from the hook), slip stitch]. This will make six points and six branches. Finally, find the chain-one space at the beginning of the round, and use a slip stitch to join into the slip stitch.

**Step 5** – You will have to block your snowflake after this. You can soak it in any stiffening solution. After some time, squeeze out the liquid and pin on a fluffy, spare towel. Keep in mind to pin the triangular points first, followed by the rectangular branches and the small loops.

Let it dry for some time. For the finishing touches, add a thread hanger into one of the loops in order to hand your snowflake on your Christmas tree or to gift it as a present.

## Beanie

A simple free crochet beanie pattern is the perfect technique to make yourself a hat. This is especially a very easy pattern to practice with and get used to if you are just getting started with crocheting. This design makes use of only two crochet stitching techniques, which are (a) the chain stitch and (b) the single crochet stitch, both of which are entry-level stitches any crocheter would be familiar with. The beanie is a classic design for a hat that is worked in the round when it comes to the design.

The equipment you will need to make this design include around 120 yards of worsted weight yarn, a yarn, a pair of scissors, and a crochet hook. Following are the instructions you need to follow step by step to design yourself a simple free crochet beanie:

**Step 1** – Make five chains using a simple slip stitch. Then, form a ring by joining them with a slip stitch.

**Step 2** – For the first round, work your way into the center of the ring, which was formed in step 1. This has to be done using ten single crochet stitches and a slip stitch to connect the first chain.

**Step 3** – Next, you will have to increase the crown. For round 2, increase the first chain by adding two single crochet stitches to the next slip stitches and repeat it ten times, working the single crochet in the joining slip stitch of the previous round. By this point, you will have 21 single crochet stitches. In rounds, 3 to 6, repeat the procedure until you have 32 stitches. Then, make a slip stitch to join the first chain with the pattern.

**Step 4** – Now, you will have to work on the body of the hate using a moss stitch pattern. This will be carried out from round 7 to all the remaining rounds. First, in round 7, join the stitches- 32 single crochet stitches with 32 chain stitches. In the next round, first, make a single crochet stitch and then a chain stitch, skip the next single crochet, and repeat the process 32 times. At the end of this round, join the pattern with the beginning point of the chain using a slip stitch. Keep repeating this process for the remaining rounds until your beanie measures approximately six and a half inches from the center of the ring you are working with, or whatever your planned measurement of depth is. In case you need to figure out whether your beanie is tall enough, you can try placing a pin through the active loop of your design and then try it on. Continue if you think you need more depth, and if it is a little too tall, undo the last few rounds you have made.

**Step 5** – In the final step of the process, fasten off your yarn while leaving around six inches of it, which will be used to weave any loose ends in. For a complete look, you can also consider blocking the crochet hat, which will be the final product of your crocheting design.

## Reusable Scrubbies

If you are a newbie to crocheting, one of the easiest things you can try creating is a reusable face scrubby. You can make one using a free crocheting pattern, and this accessory is bound to come in handy. In addition to that, making your own scrubbing is going to be both cost-efficient and eco-friendly! The process is time-efficient as well, as the entire procedure will take you less than an hour to complete.

This design will have you working your way through certain very basic crochet stitches, such as the slip stitch, the chain stitch, the half double crochet stitch, and the single crochet stitch. Follow the steps listed below to make a reusable scrubby with an estimated diameter of 2 to 3 inches:

**Step 1** – To begin with, make a slip knot and a chain. Then join both using a slip stitch, which will give you a ring.

**Step 2** – In the foundation round, form a chain by joining it with the ring using one single crochet. Repeat this six times, and use a slip stitch to join these with the first chain. By the end of this step, you must be having 12 stitches in total.

**Step 3** – Next, you need to work a couple of half double crochet stitches. Work them into each of the chain spaces, and increase the rounds by utilizing the open areas under the first chain created in the previous round. After this, form a second chain (2 half double crochets going into the next empty space, followed by a chain stitch) and repeat this procedure six times, and then join it with the first chain using a slip stitch. By the end of this step, you will now have 18 stitches.

**Step 4** – Now, you will have to increase rounds in single crochet. For round 3, use two single crochets followed by a chain stitch, and do this nine times in total. Use a slip stitch to join this chain with the first stitch. You must be having a total of 27 stitches at the end of this step.

**Step 5** – For round 4, make three chain stitches, followed by a slip stitch and single crochet in the next loop. Repeat this entire process 13 times for chain 3. Make sure to use a slip stitch as the last stitch.

Cut the yarn off next, but leave a 4-inch tail end. Next, using a tapestry needle or a yarn, carefully weave the ends in.

Now, once you have secured the ends in, you will be ready with your finished product, i.e., a reusable face scrubby. You can use leftover yarn from your other crocheting designs for this process, and this will make sure you are not wasting any of the raw material in the process! The scrubbies made this way would be easy to store as well as clean, as you can simply toss them into your laundry and send them for a wash.

## Baby Blanket

When you hear the word 'blanket,' I know what you are thinking – that it is going to take you weeks to complete it, and you will have to wait forever to see the results. But if you crochet a baby blanket and especially follow this pattern, it won't take you much time to complete it. There are only two main stitches that will be used in this project, one of them is the chain stitch, and the other one is the single crochet. And if you want to be a bit faster than usual while crocheting, use a bigger hook – it will have an additional benefit too because it will help you to add a drape to the blanket.

Even if you are a beginner, this baby blanket pattern should be easy enough for you. If you are into crocheting as a form of meditation, then too, you will find this pattern soothing. You only have to keep repeating the basic stitches over and over again until the pattern is over. So, whether you are watching your favorite TV show, waiting for your food order to arrive, or simply sitting in the car waiting for someone, this baby blanket can be done anywhere. The blanket that you will get after using this pattern will be a small one with an approximate length of 34 inches and a breadth of 26 inches.

**Step 1** – First, you have to make 105 chain stitches. To make the process easier, in the first chain from the hook, place a stitch marker. In the third chain space, make a single crochet. Then *chain one, skip next chain, single crochet in next chain*. Repeat the instructions within the asterisk throughout the row. Chain one and then turn.

**Step 2** – Next, you will be starting row two. *Make a single crochet in the next chain-one space, chain one* The sequence within the asterisk will have to be continued for the rest of the row. When you reach the end, you simply have to make a single crochet into the stitch where you had placed the marker. Once you have made the stitch, remove the marker. Chain one and then turn.

**Step 3** – All the rows that are about to come are going to be the same as Step 2, but there will be just one small difference – when you reach the end of each row, you will make the last single crochet stitch into the turning chain of the row present just before that one. Then, keep doing this until you reach the desired length of the blanket. In case you want to change colors, the same technique will be followed that you use while generally swapping colors during crocheting.

**Step 4** – Once the required length has been reached, take the yarn and cut it off, and the extra yarn left should be about six inches. Weave the yarn into the blanket with a needle. If there are any other loose ends here and there, follow the same procedure for them too.

## Wrist Warmers

When the winter season starts, our hands tend to get cold, and if they freeze, you not only feel uncomfortable but doing anything with your hands seems such a hassle. That is why I have come up with this easy and cute pattern for wrist warmers that can be customized according to your size and are very easy to make. The pattern will use treble crochet stitches, and if you are a beginner who has just learned this stitch then, I'd say that this is a perfectly good way to try it out. So, if you want a pair of fingerless gloves to keep you warm and yet you want the pattern to be fuss-free, then this is it for you.

The pattern is somewhat like this –

**Step 1** – Chain 30.

**Step 2** – Count the fourth chain from the hook and in that space make treble crochet and also in each stitch across the foundation row. After that, chain three and then turn the piece.

**Step 3** – The second step will be repeated until you reach the required size.

Now, there are certain aspects of this particular project that needs to be discussed in detail. First, let me tell you how you are going to determine the size of the gloves because that is a very important aspect of this project. So, start by first measuring what circumference your hand is or the person for whom you are making the gloves. The point of measuring will be the widest point just beside the thumb.

But you also have to keep in mind the type of yarn you are using for your project. If the yarn is a bit stretchy, then it would be best to make a pair of gloves that's one size smaller. Because when you wear those gloves, the yarn will stretch and then make it comfortable for you. But if you know that the yarn is not going to stretch much, then take the measurement carefully and make it as it is.

For reference, I will tell you what the usual sizes are –

- If you are making these for a teen or for an adult with extra small size, then the second step of the pattern will have to be repeated until it reaches a size of 6 1/8 inches.

- For a medium-size or for the standard adult size, the second step will be repeated until you reach the size of 7 inches.

- For large size, you have to make the second until 7 7/8 inches.

But even after this, just before finishing, you need to check the fit. In the active loop, attach a safety pin and then do a quick fitting test. If you think it's comfortable, then you simply have to finish the pattern. You can add one more row if it feels too tight, or you can add as many rows as you think it would need. And lastly, if you think that the fit is too tight for you, then you simply have to unravel a few of the rows or just one row.

## Pillows

The easiest and yet most beautiful way of making a pillow is by crocheting granny squares and then weaving them all together. I have already given you a granny square pattern here, and you can use it for this pillow as well. For the front of the pillow, you can use a total of nine such squares, and you can adjust the colors to your preference. After that, all the nine squares will have to be seamed together so that you get one big square.

And, for the backside of the pillow, you don't need granny squares; you only need a fabric of any color you want.

## Headband

If you are new to crocheting and you haven't made a headband yet, you need to start immediately. I can give you tons of great reasons why you should try them out. One of the best things about them is that you do not need much yarn to make them because they are small, and you can work them up very fast. They can be made for anyone you want – from small babies to adults. Moreover, the design can be adapter to your preferences – whatever design or side you want.

Here, you are going to learn the design of a wide headband that will keep your ears warm in winters. The design is somewhat tapered around the forehead, and as it goes towards the ears, it widens up. In fact, it is one of the best alternatives to any kind of winter hat. Another advantage is that if you are wearing a helmet, this headband is not going to cause any obstruction. Also, if you are out of ideas, this can be that perfect last-minute gift.

The design here will give you a finished headband of 19 inches in circumference. At the narrowest point, it is about 2-1/4 inches, and at the tallest point (which is at the back), it is about 3-1/2 inches. The center front is the region where you will start crocheting the headband and then crochet all the way to the back portion. Then, you simply have to rotate your work, and then you have to start crocheting again, and this time, it will be exactly the mirror image of the first half.

**Step 1** – First, divide the yarn into two parts (this will prevent you from weaving in any extra ends), and then, make a slip knot in the beginning. Take the small ball and make a chain 10.

**Step 2** – Now, you start your first row. Count the third chain from the hook and make a half double crochet in it and also in each chain across. The first half of the double crochet will act as the first two chains that are present in the row. In this way, you will have a total of 9 half double crochet stitches.

**Step 3** – Here is what you are going to do for Rows 2-6. Here, you have to work through the back loop only in each stitch and make a half double crochet in each of them. In this way, each row will have a total of 9 half double crochet stitches.

**Step 4** – For the 7th row, make a half double crochet in each stitch through the back loop only. When you reach the end of the row, don't forget to make two half double crochet stitches into the turning chain. This will give you a total of ten stitches in that row.

**Step 5** – For the 8th row, make a half double crochet in each stitch through the back loop only. And if you count, the total stitches in the row should be 10.

**Step 6** – For row 9, when you reach the end of the row like in Step 4, make two half double crochet stitches into the turning chain, and you will get a total of eleven stitches.

**Step 7** – In the 10th row, make a half double crochet in each stitch through the back loop only. And if you count, the total stitches in the row should be 11.

**Step 8** – For row 11, when you reach the end of the row like in Step 4, make two half double crochet stitches into the turning chain, and you will get a total of twelve stitches.

**Step 9** – For the 12th row, make a half double crochet in each stitch through the back loop only. And if you count, the total stitches in the row should be 12.

**Step 10** – For the 13<sup>th</sup> row, when you reach the end of the row like in Step 4, make two half double crochet stitches into the turning chain, and you will get a total of thirteen stitches.

**Step 11** – For the 14<sup>th</sup> row, make a half double crochet in each stitch through the back loop only. And if you count, the total stitches in the row should be 14.

**Step 12** – For the 15<sup>th</sup> row, when you reach the end of the row like in Step 4, make two half double crochet stitches into the turning chain, and you will get a total of 14 stitches.

**Step 13** – For rows 16-20, make a half double crochet in each stitch through the back loop only. And if you count, the total stitches in the row should be 14.

Here, the rows can be adjusted depending on the size of the headband. In the active loop, attach a safety pin, rotate your work to make the other side, and return to your starting chain.

**Step 14** – For the 21<sup>st</sup> row, take the other ball of yarn, pull up a loop with your hook and then, chain two. From the starting chain, work backward, and in each free loop across the row, make one half double crochet. The total number of stitches will be nine.

For rows 22-26, you simply have to repeat what you did for rows 2-6.

**Step 15** – For the 27<sup>th</sup> row, you have to make one stitch extra in the beginning. And for this, make two half double crochet stitches into the back loop of the first stitch. In this way, you will have to make an increase throughout the pattern. The rest of the stitches are simply a mirror image of the first half.

**Step 16 -** After you each row 40, it is time to finish the headband. Take the two ends of the headband, hold them together, and use a slip stitch to join them. Weave the ends in, and your headband is ready!

## Cellphone Bag

This is a cozy, simple crochet pattern that will help you make a cellphone bag, and it can be customized to the shape of your phone. And all you need to know are four basic crochet stitches – treble crochet, double crochet, half double crochet, and single crochet.

**Step 1 –** Chain 11.

**Step 2 –** Here is what you will do for the first row. Count the second chain from the hook and in it, make a single crochet and also in each subsequent chain that follows. Total stitches = 10

**Step 3 –** In the 2nd row, turn the piece, chain one (your first single crochet), single crochet in the next stitch, and each stitch that follows.

**Step 4 –** In the 3rd row, you are going to repeat step 3.

**Step 5 –** In the 4th row, turn, chain two (your first double crochet), double crochet in the next stitch, and in every stitch that follows.

**Step 6 –** In rows 5-6, repeat Step 5.

**Step 7 –** In the 7th row, turn, chain 3 (your first treble crochet), treble crochet in the next stitch, and in every stitch across the row.

**Step 8** – For rows 8-9, repeat Step 7.

**Step 9** – For the 10th row, turn, chain two (your first half double crochet), half double crochet in the next stitch, and in every stitch across that row.

**Step 10** – For rows 11-12, repeat Step 9.

**Step 11** – For rows 13-15, repeat Step 7.

**Step 12** – For rows 16-18, repeat Step 5.

**Step 13** – For rows 19-21, repeat Step 3.

**Step 14** – For finishing, fold the piece in the middle so that you get the half double crochets along the folding line. The two long sides will have to be seamed up, and your case is ready.

## Coaster

Here, I will be giving you the simplest coasters that you can make by crocheting. But the challenge is to make a flat coaster and not something that will be wonky. The method shown here is quite easy and quick and perfect for a beginner.

**Step 1** – Make a slip knot to begin and then form two chain stitches. Coun the 2nd chain from the hook, and then make six single crochet stitches into that chain. To join at the end of the round, make a slip stitch.

**Step 2** – Now, we come to the second round of your coaster. In each that you already made in the previous step, you are going to make two single crochet stitches. In this way, for round two, you will have a total of twelve single crochet stitches. In order to join, make a slip stitch to the 1st stitch.

**Step 3** – Moving on to the 3rd round of your coaster – for the next stitch, you will make two single crochet stitches. After that, you have to make one stitch and then two stitches and keep alternating like this. If you keep doing this for the entire circle, your round will end with you having a total of eighteen single crochet stitches. Join with the first stitch using a slip stitch.

**Step 4** – Now, we move on to the 4th round of this crochet. For the next stitch, we use a single crochet stitch. Then, in the following stitch, we make another single crochet stitch. In the next stitch, you make two single crochet stitches. This pattern will have to be repeated throughout the circumference of the circle and then when you reach the end, join with the help of a slip stitch.

**Step 5** – You can continue with the same pattern if you want to grow the circle. The only difference is that before you make the two single crochet stitches, you have to add one more single crochet in each round. For example, let us say that you are continuing to the 5th round. Then, in the 1st three stitches, you will make one single crochet stitch, and then in the next stitch, you will make two single crochets in the same stitch. Similarly, in the 6th round, in the 1st four stitches, you will make one single crochet stitch, and then in the next stitch, you will make two single crochet stitches in the same stitch.

As soon as you feel that the coaster is large enough for you, you can end your circle. And, in case you want to give this project a more finished look, then make slip stitches all around the circle, and it will have the perfect edging.

# Chapter 6: Care Instructions For the Yarn

The utmost extroverted and general expression of love is to gift the person we love with some hand made products. Many of us love knitting and hence gift knitted products. Yarn products are an emotion. We all get overjoyed on receiving a knitted product, do not we? It does not necessarily have to be a gift; we love buying knitted products.

Blankets, sweaters, socks, throw covers, beanies, shawls, bags – everything that is made with yarn, have warmth in them, and a feeling of love. Some of us directly link these products with our childhood memories when our mothers or grandparents would sit for days and knit that favorite sweater or beanie for us that goes on to become our favorite. No matter which part of the country or world a person lives in, everyone has at least one memory of crochet products.

However, taking care of yarns, washing them, and maintaining them can be intimidating. The fear of destroying the material or wearing them out in the process of cleaning it may take away all the happiness. But it is not that difficult if you trust us. Crochet products are very much washable and can be cleaned easily without reshaping or damaging them. With proper care and maintenance, these threads of love can be used for a greater period. Continue reading to learn about the proper cleaning, drying, maintaining, and all other care instructions for yarn.

## Learn to Wash Your Crochet Products Properly

The proper method of washing plays a key role in maintaining crochet. So here is everything that you need to know and keep in mind while washing yarns.

### How Frequently Shall We Wash Our Crochet or Knit Product?

Heavy woolen blankets or sweaters, or any other product do not need frequent washing. Most products that are worn over other clothing items do not need washing after every single wear. They can be washed once or twice at max throughout the season.

Frequent washing harms the product more than anything. Unless and until necessary, avoid washing any knitted product. Instead, you can just dust them off and lay them under the sun.

### Read the Care Labels Carefully

The easiest way to know about how to wash the yarn is to read the care labels. Most crochet items come with care instructions, which also include the proper method of washing. Different types of yarns require different types of washing, and to know which washing technique is best suited for the yarn in your hand; you have to figure out the type of the item. This may not always be possible; reading the care labels is a quick fix.

Major crochet brands provide a blurb as well as an online manual for washing the products. There are major symbols, like ironing, dry clean, tumble drying, and handwashing, and an 'X' on them implies that those measures must be avoided for that particular product. If the blurb does not provide ample washing related information, then read their online websites.

**Proper Methods of Washing and Drying Yarns**

The best way of washing crochet is to hand wash them with mild detergents. To wash your favorite crochet product properly, follow the steps mentioned below –

- Take a bucket and fill it with a proper amount of water. Make sure the water is cold and not smoking. Hot water can cause the yarn to loosen up and thus make it saggy and thin.

- Add mild detergent to a bucket of water. If possible, use fabric softeners! Fabric Softeners not only softens your yarn but also ensures your loved product is kept from pilling. They reduce static friction in the knit, thus help to keep the product new for a longer period. Gently swirl the item, and avoid using brushes or anything that includes rubbing it.

- If indeed you must machine launder your yarn, you must wash it with a minimum number of clothes. If possible, wash the item alone. More number of items together in the machine cause more rubbing, thus more friction. Friction is bad for yarns, which temporarily lose their tensile strength during friction, and the smaller fabrics readily separate from the rest—thus causing wear and tear of the delicate item.

- Another measure that can be taken for machine laundering is placing the yarn inside a cotton or mesh bag and then giving it for washing. This decreases the rubbing of the yarn with other items and also prevents them from attracting small fibers to themselves.

- Dry the product in minimum possible heat, even if it takes a longer time to dry. The proper way of drying your knitted product is to first squeeze it to get rid of all the excess water. Then, wrap it in a soft cloth to soak in the remaining water. It should then be laid out flat on a smooth surface to dry it completely.

Note that you must never hang it in the clothing line. Water makes the yarn heavy, and then hanging them will pull the yarn, making it lose its tensile strength. Thus, leading the water-saturated product stretched, lose its shape, and make it look old. This state is maintained even after it dries out.

Avoid laying the product directly under the sun; this might cause the color of the yarn to burn out. If at all, then flip it inside out and then place it under the sun.

Crochet is delicate, and machine washing them can lead to wearing of the material, so try and handwash them whenever possible.

# Storing Instructions for Your Yarn

Before storing your yarn, make sure it is completely dry. It is strictly mentioned even in most of the blurbs that come along with the product that it should never be stuffed away while it is still moist.

Place soft and smooth fabrics inside each fold of the yarn to avoid friction, which is undesirable for the fabric (explained in detail in the next section). Also, place smooth cloth or tissues under and over the yarn to avoid rubbing and sticking of other fabrics placed above and below.

Make sure to never hang your yarn for the same reason as mentioned in the earlier sections. Hanging stretches out the product, making it lose its original shape.

## Remove Pills from Knitted Clothes or Blankets

Pilling is the formation of small balls on the outer or inner surface of the knitted product. Pilling can pull down the overall look of the garment or blanket or carpet and make it look dull and worn out. People usually chose to stop using a yarn product once it starts pilling or throws them away. But with proper care and the right technique of removing the pills, you can depill your favorite knitted item in no time and make it look new.

Pilling is one of the main reasons why a certain section of people refrain from using them. To be honest, pilling can be hard to avoid. It occurs due to friction from normal usage of the garment or frequent washing and cleaning of the same. It may also occur due to the loosening of the yarn product. This causes the length and the shorter fibers to separate from one another, resulting in the shorter fibers freeing themselves from the major product and forming short frizz balls.

These clumps start getting more and more pronounced with more usage. As these become more prominent, small pieces of fabric and lints start sticking to it, deteriorating the condition further. You cannot avoid pilling as these occur in areas of maximum friction. For example, in yarn sweaters, pilling can occur in the underarm region, elbow area due to the resting of elbow on desks or any surface, inside region of the arms due to friction between arms and the material, and collars. In woolen pants, pilling occurs in insightful areas due to constant sitting on chairs.

Do not worry; pilling may seem inevitable in natural yarns, but minimizing and complete removal of them is possible. Few steps that can be taken to avoid or minimize pilling in yarn products are

- As already mentioned above, try hand washing your product instead of dry cleaning it or machine washing it unless and until required or mentioned in the instruction manual.

- Sticking of fabrics or lints in the affected areas leads to worsening of the condition. So to avoid such happening, flip your product while putting it for washing, if you have to machine launder the item.

- Avoid unnecessary rubbing of the yarn product to reduce abrasion and thus minimizing the chances of pilling.

If these clump balls still occur on your product, which is very likely, then here are a few tools that can be used for de-pilling.

- Sweater shavers

- Velcro, only the face with hooks to be used

- Scissors (the most common household technique of removing pills from woolen winter garments)

- Safety razors chose disposable ones

- Fine grit commercial sandpaper

- Depilling combs – specially built to remove pills from natural or synthetic fiber products or garments and have very fine-toothed combs. These should be mainly used for clothes

- Sweater stone

Printed in Great Britain
by Amazon

40801120R00057